THE SIAMESE KITTENS AND THE BREADCRUMBS

Also by Michael Haykin & Chris Iliff
Reformation Lightning

The Siamese Kittens and the Snow Leopard
The Siamese Kittens and the Christmas Hedgehog

THE SIAMESE KITTENS AND THE BREADCRUMBS

Michael A.G. Haykin
Illustrated by Chris Iliff

Reformation
Lightning

First published in Great Britain in 2023

British Library Cataloguing in Publication Data
A record for this book is available from the British Library

ISBN: 978-1-916669-03-1

Designed and typeset by Pete Barnsley (CreativeHoot.com)
Illustrated by Chris Iliff (ChrisIliff.co.uk)

Printed in Denmark

Reformation Lightning, an imprint of 10Publishing
Unit C, Tomlinson Road, Leyland, PR25 2DY, England

Email: info@10ofthose.com
Website: www.10ofthose.com

1 3 5 7 10 8 6 4 2

1

THE KITTENS

It was a windy day in March when Mr. Quinn brought the three kittens, Siam and Ko-ko and Java, home to his old country house near Dublin.

Up the long driveway he came in his car with the three kittens on the backseat. Their names suited them well, for they were Siamese kittens and their ancestors had come from the country of Thailand, which a long time ago had once been called Siam. And, like all Siamese cats, they loved to think they came from royalty.

Whether they did, or not, I cannot say, but they thought they did and sometimes they would prance around like kings and queens. But right now, all three were sitting still in the car and mewing quite loudly. They didn't like riding in cars.

Like all Siamese cats, the three kittens were very talkative. They would tell anyone who wanted to listen all about their day – how it was going, how much they had slept (as you know, cats love to sleep), what they had eaten and what they wanted for dinner. They simply loved to talk. They were especially talkative when they were upset – as they were now. They would mew and mew and mew till they made people's heads ache!

But, of course, they just wanted whatever was bothering them to be made right.

Java

Well, as soon as they came to a complete stop at the end of the driveway, the kittens started feeling better. Mr. Quinn brought them into the house and introduced them to his family – his wife, Mrs. Quinn, and his four children, who crowded around the kittens and said they were so cute and so lovely. The kittens knew they were going to like living in this house.

Siam, Ko-ko and Java were sisters and brother. Both sisters, Siam and Ko-ko, had deep chocolate brown ears with black noses and dark velvet paws, but Java was a ginger color with a fine pink nose, lovely furry orange

stripes on his forehead, and orange-colored paws. Being ginger meant that sometimes Java was mistaken for being a common tabby cat – and that would upset him. "Oh, what a lovely tabby cat," people would sometimes say, bending down to pet him. He would immediately stop purring and begin to mew. Loudly.

He was not a tabby, he would tell them, he was a royal Siamese cat.

Actually, in Java's mind, he liked to think he was related to that lovely big cat, the tiger. When Java looked at himself in a mirror, he would see the stripes on his forehead and think that he was a big, fierce tiger. He would try to roar at his sisters to scare them, just like a tiger's roar, but they knew that he was just their lovable little brother, and they

wouldn't be scared at all. Siam and Ko-ko would tell him to stop being silly and that he only had a few stripes on his forehead, not his entire body. They knew that he was not a tiger.

His roar was not loud at all (and certainly not scary).

In no time at all, the kittens began sniffing around, rubbing themselves on the furniture and jumping all over the Quinns, who laughed with delight. Despite that horrible drive, the kittens began to feel that they would enjoy their new home after all…

2

CHAI

There was another member
of the big Irish house that Siam,
Ko-ko and Java had yet to meet.
Another cat named Chai.

He too was a Siamese cat, and he was much older than our three kittens; twelve summers had come and gone since he was a kitten like them and, to be honest, Chai was getting a little chubby (although he was glad of the warmth when it was cold).

He had once raced around the house which had kept him sleek and slender like our three kittens. But now he was getting older and, instead of running, he liked to watch the comings and goings while he munched on his favourite nibbles.

Chai was not related to our kittens, but, after giving them a sniff, Chai decided that he would take care of them. After all, they had come to the house when they were very young. They were spunky and full of fun, and they reminded him of how he had once been.

So, he taught them the ways of the house: where the comfiest spots were to sleep, where best to bask in the sun, where the most fun places to explore were, how to cuddle together in wintertime, and where not to go – the edge of the bathtub, for example, when it was filled with water!

Once, he had fallen into a bathtub full of water. One of Mr. Quinn's sons had left the water in the bath while he was drying himself. And Chai, trying to leap from one side of the tub to the other, had landed right in the middle with a big loud

Plop! Sploosh!

He went into the water and the soapsuds, feet first. Mrs. Quinn had rescued him, but he was so embarrassed and dripping wet from the tip of his pinkish nose to the very end of his jet-black tail. It was horrible to have his nice fur so bedraggled. And from that day on, he stayed away from the bathrooms when the children were having their baths.

But, perhaps most importantly, Chai taught them about the foods he loved to eat. And

Chai liked to eat. Maybe this was one reason why he was a little chubby. He had his kibbles and cat food that the Quinns gave him. But his all-time favourite food was people-food.

First, there were sardines and all things fishy. He filled the heads of Siam and Ko-ko and Java with so many mouth-watering stories about eating fish that he soon had them licking their lips with their tiny tongues. Then there was yogurt. Mrs. Quinn enjoyed having a bowl of yogurt now and then. And when she had finished, she would let Chai lick the bowl. Chai told our three kittens that strawberry yogurt tasted the yummiest. Of course, Chai would not touch or even lick a real live strawberry, but strawberry yogurt was quite different – it was so delicious! Do you like yogurt?

Chai even loved the milky tea that Mr. and Mrs. Quinn left in their mugs. When they had finished drinking their tea, Chai would check to see if there was any left and, if there was, he loved to slurp it down. I suppose it must have been the milk he loved because who ever heard of cats liking tea?

With Chai as their teacher, our three kittens were soon doing the same. But if there was one thing that Chai really loved to eat, it was breadcrumbs for breakfast.

3

THE BREADCRUMBS

You might think it odd for a Siamese cat to love crumbs from bread, and it was. But Chai was no ordinary cat. And, as it turned out, neither were Siam and Ko-ko and Java.

When one of the Quinn family would put two slices of bread in the toaster, Chai and the kittens would catch a whiff and come running from wherever they had been. Nothing was more important than yummy breadcrumbs – even the constant grooming they did to their fur to keep themselves looking like the royals they thought they were.

Of course, not all breadcrumbs were the same. There were crumbs from whole wheat bread and from flax seed bread, and even from what the Quinns called ancient grains bread, which the kittens tolerated – "ancient" sounded very old to our young kittens!

But what they really loved were crumbs from ordinary white bread. The Quinns went to a special bakery for this particular bread.

One day, the kittens awoke to the slam of the front door. The Quinns had gone out. Siam and Ko-ko and Java yawned, stretched, and scrambled over each other in their race to the kitchen. Their stomachs were growling for their usual fill of breadcrumbs. But when they slid across the kitchen tiles, they were horrified to see that there was no bread toasting in the toaster after all.

Usually, the Quinns would break off bits of the toasted bread crust onto a plate and then put it down for Chai and the Siamese kittens to eat. You should see them eating those breadcrumbs. You would think they hadn't eaten for a week!

It would only take a few moments for the plates to be lapped clean and for Chai and the kittens to be licking their lips for more. If they were really lucky, the breadcrumbs would sometimes have flecks of jam or peanut butter. Java particularly loved those bits. Blackcurrant jam was his all-time favourite and peanut butter was simply heavenly.

But today, the kittens began to worry. Would there be no breadcrumbs for breakfast? Surely not. They decided to search every corner of the room to see if Mr. and Mrs. Quinn had left them any on a forgotten plate. Siam even poked her head into the big fireplace that had once been used for cooking and came out with spider webs on her chocolate-coloured ears. There was nothing there.

Suddenly, Ko-Ko had a not-so-nice thought. She looked at the others, her tail drooping.

"What if there are never ever any more crumbs?"

4

TRUST

A seed of panic began to form in the kittens' young heads.

"Perhaps they've hidden the breadcrumbs in the house?" Java suggested after his stomach gave a particularly loud gurgle. It was a silly idea really, but the kittens, not used to such feelings of worry and not knowing what else to do, felt compelled to check.

They bounded through the hallways of the old Irish country-house. Siam went into a big room with many chairs and a massive window that looked out over a large body of water. This water was called a Bay and the water in it came from the Irish Sea. Mr. and Mrs. Quinn and their children would sometimes sit and just look at the water. Siam thought this was a bit weird. She didn't like bodies of water like the Bay and could not figure out why her

owners did. Nevertheless, she used her paws to check behind the chairs. No breadcrumbs.

Java pretended he was a big, fierce tiger as he looked in all the bedrooms, bathrooms, and closets. Tigers weren't afraid. But he tried to be particularly careful in the closets as all three kittens sometimes found themselves locked in. This was a real problem for Ko-ko. Her mew was so quiet that sometimes when she got locked in a closet, she could not raise her voice loud enough to be heard and rescued.

You might think this very sad, but if Siam and Java saw she was missing for any length of time, they would find her by using their noses and sense of smell, and so help Mr. Quinn or one of his family rescue her. Java searched high and low and eventually pulled out buttons, beads, and other bits-and-bobs. But no breadcrumbs.

Ko-ko went straight to the library. It was her favourite room, so surely Mr. Quinn – who often sat in there reading – would know to leave breadcrumbs there. She began to climb up the shelves as she loved to climb and knew it would give her the best view of the entire room. As she climbed, she remembered how she would sometimes go too high and would have to mew and mew till Mr. or Mrs. Quinn came and lifted her down to the ground. She also remembered how fun it was to go behind the shelves and use her little black nose to push and push and push until the books fell off. She loved the big sound they would make as they hit the floor. But if Mr. Quinn caught her doing it, he would tell her, "No, we don't do that, Ko-ko." Today however, Ko-Ko only knocked a few books off by accident. She was determined to find her breadcrumbs (and she didn't want to upset Mr. Quinn). But despite her best efforts, she couldn't see or smell even a whiff of grain, flax-seed or jam.

No breadcrumbs!

By this point, the kittens were very anxious indeed. Together again, the kitchen began to fill with their mewing.

"What if the bakery is no longer baking bread?" "What if the Quinns no longer like toast?" they yowled to each other. "What if the Quinns forget about us?"

Chai, who had seen many crumb-less days before, was still sleeping. He was curled up on the kitchen window ledge, enjoying the heat and warmth of the morning sunlight. But the racket the young cats were making soon pulled him from his dreams.

"Whatever's the matter?" He yawned, rubbing himself against them to help ease their trembling. Drawing close, they explained.

“Not to worry,” Chai said. He told them that sometimes the crumbs did not appear, but eventually in a day or so, the crumbs would be there.

As I said, Chai was no ordinary cat. And he was very, very wise. Over the many years he had lived in the Quinns' old house, he had learned two important things: the Quinns loved him, and they loved toast. The crumbs would be there sooner or later.

And sure enough, a few hours later with the jangle of keys in the lock, he was right.

"He provides … bread that
sustains human hearts" … and cats

Psalm 104:14–15

ACKNOWLEDGEMENTS

Thanks to great friends who read this book in manuscript form and gave feedback: Justin Taylor, Molli Benge, Sara Woods, Caroline Wilsey, Lydia Weaver, Katherine Grace Weaver, Jack Clary, Molly Clary, Kate Clary, and Tom Clary.